Sasquatch
The Native Truth

© Melissa George 2016

All rights reserved. No part of this publication may be reproduced, distributed, or transmitted in any form or by any means, including photocopying, copying, downloading, uploading, recording, or other electronic or mechanical methods, without the prior written permission of the publisher and/or Author.

Although the author and publisher have made every effort to ensure that the information in this book was correct at press time, the author and publisher do not assume and hereby disclaim any liability to any party for any loss, damage, or disruption caused by errors or omissions, whether such errors or omissions result from negligence, accident, or any other cause.

Cover Illustration Copyright © 2016 by Melissa George / Melisssa George Media

Cover design Melissa George Media

Book design and production by Southern Moon Publishing

ISBN-13:
978-1523735686

ISBN-10:
1523735686

This is NOT a work of fiction, however the Author has chosen to change names and places in the book to keep the identity of herself and her family private. We respect this right. Any names and locations used within this book are purely fictitious.

I dedicate this book to my sister Rain.
May Gods rays of sun,
shine down on your upturned face.
While the fingers of the wind
Comb through your hair.
May you find the peace
within your soul,
that you knew as a child.
And may your voice once again
make the morning song birds jealous.

When Melissa approached me to tell my story, I was warned by my people that I should not do this. I was told that there would be repercussions for telling my story. I thought long and hard about this, and I feel the truth should be told. Melissa assured me that there was a way to tell my story and still protect my identity, and the identity of my people. Any names and locations used within this book are fictitious. The story and the encounters are true. It needs to be said, it needs to be told. People need to be warned. They are out there, and they are watching you.

Chapter 1

I was just ten years old in the spring of 1974. My father and I were getting ready to go fishing. It was early in the morning and still quite chilly. The rest of the family were still asleep as I watched my dad pour steaming hot coffee into a thermos bottle. I loved it when my dad and I got to spend time together. Usually, my younger sister Rain tagged along. But today it would be just me and my dad.

My father, Matt, was a large man, standing six foot four and about two hundred and fifty pounds. He had the dark hair and dark eyes of our ancestors. He had a gentle nature and an easy smile. He was easy to laugh, but just as easy to give a firm hand if needed. The village council respected him for his honest nature and love of the old ways.

Dad still honored the old tradition that we would live off the land. He believed that hard work and mother nature were all you needed to survive. We trapped, hunted and fished for our meat and our vegetables came from the garden. The fruit we enjoyed came from mama's fruit trees. This is the way I was raised, so to me, this was the way it was supposed to be. Most people on the Rez (reservation) grew their own gardens, but not to the extinct that we did.

They supplemented their gardens with grocery shopping in town. This is something we rarely did. All of our food came from our land.

Now don't get me wrong. We weren't like some of these people you see on TV that live way out in the middle of nowhere chiseling out a life for themselves and living solely off the land. We lived in the mountains and yes, it was very rural. But a drive into town gave us a movie theater and fast food restaurants just like any other place in small town America. Our reservation covered the town and a good part of the neighboring mountain region. That is where we were. Mom and dad liked the privacy and that was fine with me. We had electricity and water just like everyone else. We had a TV and telephone, but there were no computers and cell phones back then so we didn't miss it. TV was usually watched at night as a family and then the Saturday morning cartoons that my sister and I enjoyed. Mom kept a small radio on in the kitchen and usually had it tuned to some country station as she worked. There were times I would sit on the back steps and listen to her sing along. Mom had a beautiful singing voice. Dad would say that she should have been named Sparrow.

We lived in a two-story cabin. Mom said that dad built it all by hand with the help of his brothers, Luke and John.

There were times I would look around and be amazed that my dad did all of this. He had cut all of the trees himself, giving him the wood to build our home and clearing the land for our farm in the process.

The kitchen was large, so mom would have plenty of room for cooking, baking and canning. In the summer months, there was always something cooking on the stove getting ready for her quart jars. I didn't mind helping her, but with no air conditioner, it sure was hot work.

Our Mom, Paula, was as much of a hard worker as dad was. She didn't believe in sitting around all day with your nose shoved in a book. Which was something Rain and I loved to do. Mom was a short lady, barely standing five foot three. She had the light olive skin of her heritage along with the large waistline. Mom came from a different tribe than my father, yet a lot of their beliefs were the same. You got by with hard work and prayer. Our mother was soft spoken and had a constant smile. She too had the dark hair and eyes that were common to any Native American. She kept her long hair braided then wrapped in a tight bun on her head. I loved to watch her brush it out, it was the same blue-black of a raven's wing.

The living room was also large with a huge fireplace covering one wall.

Dad had hauled all of the rocks up from the river to make it. Sometimes in the winter, we would cook dinner over the fire. I enjoyed it when mom did this. It made me feel like our ancestors were close by watching over us. In the fall, they would allow me and my sister, Rain, to pop fresh popcorn. It always tasted better when cooked over the fire.

My sister Rain was only a year younger than me, so she and I spent most of our time together. She was shorter than me and looked a lot like our mother. I had taken after our father with the long legs and slim build. A lot of people at school could never guess that we were sisters. We teased one another about being from different tribes like our parents.

Dad had filled the thermos and now was wrapping a couple of the buttermilk biscuits we had left over from dinner last night. These would be enjoyed later this morning while we were fishing.

We headed across the yard toward the trail that led down to the river. The sun hadn't started to rise yet and the morning silence made it seem as if the whole world was still asleep. The only sound was our footsteps crunching the frozen leaves. As we made our way across the big yard, the barn was to our left, some of the horses heard us and gave sleepy snorts.

We passed the goat fence that was completely empty. At this hour, they were all still in their shelter. As we neared the head of the trail the surrounding woods looked dark and scary. I had grown up playing in these woods, but only during the daylight hours. Mom and Dad warned us not to go near the woods at night. There were too many dangerous animals out there. And the Kecleh-Kudleh hunted at night. The Kecleh-Kudleh was our native tongue for "Hairy Savage", meaning Bigfoot or Sasquatch. The Kecleh-Kudleh was a very large creature that roamed the forest at night. The woods and land had belonged to them way before us, so we owed them a certain amount of respect. There were even stories of children and small animals being taken by the Kecleh-Kudleh. As we neared the woods, I walked a little closer to my father and pulled my hood up tightly over my head. The air was still cold, so the warm hooded coat felt good and I felt more protected from anything that might be watching us.

I knew that monsters weren't real. And I assumed the elders just made up these stories so they didn't have to worry about us kids getting lost in the woods. Even with knowing this, I was glad to have my Dad leading the way.

We neared the first trap and dad handed me his fishing rod and had me wait on the trail as he entered the woods to check it.

I wasn't at all comfortable with this, but I didn't let on. I couldn't have my dad thinking I was spooked he might not ask me to come with him next time. As I stood there alone on the trail I listened to my dad's footsteps walking away until I could no longer hear them. In the eerie silence, a branch snapped to my right causing me to jump and spin around. I couldn't see anything as the early morning light was not strong enough yet to penetrate the inky darkness. It could have been a squirrel landing on a dead branch. I strained my ears but didn't hear anything else.

I stood there for what seemed like forever. Why was it taking dad so long? Maybe he was having a hard time freeing the animal. I could have gone with him, but I wouldn't have been much help. I wasn't old enough to carry a knife on my side just yet. But dad had said maybe by next season. Then I would get to really help dad with checking the traps.

 I stood there in the dark thinking about all of the stories I had heard. What if the Kecleh-Kudleh were watching me? What if they didn't want us in the woods? Another branch broke and my heart began to pound. I wished the sun would hurry up so the woods wouldn't be so dark. I had never been in the woods alone in the dark and I didn't like it at all. I was thinking about all of the scary stories the kids told at school. Standing here alone in the dark woods made them seem more real now than ever.

"Look what I've got" came dad's voice. The sudden noise in the silence caused my adrenaline to surge through my veins. I turned to see dad coming back out of the woods holding up a white snow rabbit. 'This will make a mighty fine stew tonight," he said.

He sat his backpack down on the trail and opened it to drop the rabbit in. I saw that he had already bled it and cleaned it out. That must have been what took him so long.

He slung his pack over one shoulder and his gun over the other. He turned to me to get his fishing rod and stopped. He was looking up the trail past me. I could tell by the look on his face that he had seen something. I turned to look at what he was seeing. There was nothing on the trail. I could only see about twenty yards, then the trail turned left into the woods. "What did you see?" I asked

"Oh, nothing", dad answered, "I had thought it was another rabbit".

I didn't get the feeling that he was being totally honest with me. I knew he had seen something. But why wouldn't he tell me what it was? What was the big deal I wondered. I was familiar with all of the wildlife around here.

"Let's go," he said, as he began walking. 'We still have a few more traps to check before we get to the river".

The next few traps were empty. The ones that had been triggered dad re-baited, but, this time, I tramped through the woods with him. I wasn't being left alone like I had earlier. Something had my nerves on edge.

As we followed the trail on down, the frozen dew had begun to melt, leaving wet leaves and causing some of the areas to become slippery. I had started paying more attention to my footing than the surrounding woods. I didn't want to fall and get my coat damp or possibly break my fishing rod.

The morning had begun to get colder just before the sun come up. Dad and I both looked like steam engines with our breath coming out in white plumes. I pulled my coat a little closer around me enjoying the warmth it provided.

I was beginning to hear the water rushing over the falls to our far right. We wouldn't be going anywhere near the falls today. We had a better spot about a half a mile up the river. It was a nice and calm area of water, that usually provided a lot of fish. We arrived at our spot just as the sun topped the mountain.

I stood there relishing the beauty of the purples, orange and yellow that the sun was creating in the clouds. I spoke a silent prayer to our creator in giving thanks for such beauty.

The river was wider here and the water was calmer. The trees on the far bank were thick with Mountain Laurel. Sometimes Rain and I would go to a spot further up the river. There was a nice sandy area where we could walk the horses right into the water. It didn't have the drop off bank like this one did. That's what made this one better for catching fish. They would hide in the grasses against the bank along with the bugs and baby fish they like to eat. Looking across the river, it occurred to me that I had never explored the far bank, but I was thinking this summer might be a good time to do that. I would bring my sister Rain up here with me. She would enjoy that.

"It sure is pretty. Isn't it"? Dad asked. Bringing me out of my daydream.

I looked over to see him admiring the sunrise as well.

"Uh Huh," I agreed.

"Well, let's get these rods baited and in the water," he said

Dad had a large rock right by where he sat that he would prop his gun on. It had been here as far back as I could remember. I'm not sure if dad put it there, or if it was natural, but it was the perfect place for him to prop up his gun within easy reach while we fished.

It wasn't long before Dad and I had a nice stringer full. We took a break to enjoy the coffee and biscuits he had brought. I had finished eating and was lying on the bank enjoying the feel of the warm sun when a large branch snapped in the woods behind us. Dad immediately jumped to his feet, grabbed his gun and spun around. The sudden loud noise had sent adrenaline surging through my veins. I knew dad was expecting to see a bear coming out of the woods lured in by the smell of our morning catch. We waited, holding our breath and straining our ears, knowing he would break the tree line any second. This wouldn't be the first time a bear had wanted to challenge dad for fish. The last one's head hung over the fireplace.

After a few minutes of not hearing or seeing anything, dad propped his gun against the rock he had been resting it on and began to pack our things back into his backpack.
"I guess it's getting time for us to head back", he said.

This struck me as odd, we would usually fish well past lunch time and sometimes right on into the early evening. The fish had been biting. I didn't understand why he would want to leave.

"Head back?" I asked

"Yes", said dad. "I have some things at home to get done today".

I stood up and looked to the edge of the woods. We kept an old bucket hanging here for cleaning the fish. I was wondering if it was safe for me to approach the tree line.

As if reading my mind, dad said, "Let them be today".

Was he not wanting me to clean the fish? But why? This is something we always did before we started home unless, it was already dark. And I could clean them almost as good as he could.

'What"? I said. More than a little confused.

We'll take care of them at the house dad said.
"Get your stuff together and come on."

I bent down and gathered my things, then ran to catch up with dad. He was already at the trail head waiting for me. I was feeling really confused at the events of the day. This just wasn't normal. We had never stopped fishing this early, especially when they were biting so good. I had thought that dad seemed a little uneasy today. I didn't know exactly what was wrong. I was only ten years old, but I could tell when something just wasn't right. And dad's behavior wasn't normal. It made me nervous to see dad acting so unpredictable.

Possibly picking up on my confusion, dad said, "Your Uncle Luke said there had been a rogue bear in the area lately and I don't want to take any chances." That explained it! There was a bear in the near vicinity. Having a rogue near meant that we weren't safe out here. Especially carrying a mess of fish. Now I understood why dad had appeared jumpy and ready to leave early. I was ready to leave now!

I grabbed my fishing rod and hurried up the trail behind him. We hadn't gone too far when dad stopped walking signaling for me to listen. I stopped instantly, holding my breath. I didn't dare make a sound. Dad had heard something and was trying to make out what it was. He slowly bent down and sat his pack on the ground. Then he slid his gun from his shoulder. I quietly knelt down behind him.

I was looking around dads leg, in the same direction he was. But I didn't see a thing in the trees. Nothing at all was moving. Then I heard it, another loud branch snap and a very low rumble. It sounded almost like a growl, but the sound was so low that it was almost inaudible. My heart began to pound and sweat popped out on my forehead. A bear! We were being flanked by a bear! I froze in place, not hearing anything but the pounding of my own heart. I knew dad had his gun, but that didn't make us completely safe. A rogue bear that was hunting in close proximity to humans could be very dangerous.

I had seen bears in the distance. But I had never had an encounter with one. Dad raised his gun and used the scope to search for any movement. After a few minutes, I knew the threat was gone as he once again shouldered his gun and picked up his pack. He turned to look at me.

" I want you to walk in front of me, and we're going to pick up the pace just a little. If at any time you feel my hand on your shoulder, I want you to freeze. Got it"?

I quickly nodded my head and stepped up in front of dad. This had never happened before and it made my blood run cold to see my dad so concerned. I did just as Dad had told me and walked as fast as I could without running.

We kept hearing branches break as if the bear flanked us all the way back to our yard. Once we broke the tree line I breathed a sigh of relief. A bear was less likely to walk right out in the open yard and challenge you.

Dad and I went around to the back side of the barn where he would clean the fish. This barn had been here as far back as I could remember. It had two massive doors on each end with a large breezeway down the center. The inside housed a tack room and four horses, one for each of us. Meredith was mine, Thunder belonged to dad, Rain had Lady bug and mom had Lucky. I loved it when we all went riding together. We had four milk cows that dad sometimes moved in there during the winter months.

I loved the smell of this old barn. It smelled of hay, horses and old wood. Rain and I played in here during the summer months when it was just too hot to be outside. When all of the doors were open, the wind would blow right through the center, creating a nice place to play while offering a reprieve from the heat.

Dad had an old wood table set up just to the left of the barn doors. This is where he worked on the horseshoes, built fence posts and anything else that needed doing. I went around to the side of the house to get him a fresh bucket of water.

I took the bucket off the hook and set it down under the spigot. I turned the nozzle and fresh clear water started filling the bucket. Sometimes in the summer, he would connect a hose pipe here and allow Rain and me to spray each other.

I took the water back around the barn to dad's table. He had already begun the messy job of cleaning the fish. He would scale them and cut the heads off, then he would slice the meat away from the bone creating a thick filet.

I watched as his skilled hands ran through each fish with precision. Dad had done this for many years, so his knife flew through what would have been a job for me. I watched as the scales and heads were tossed into a bucket at his feet. This bucket would then be taken down to the far edge of the yard, just at the tree line and set on a tree stump for the wildlife. This was always something dad had done himself. As far back as I could remember, this bucket had been sat on that stump every evening.

He finished with the fish and placed the fillets in the clean bucket of water.

"You take these on up to your mama," he said handing me the bucket of clean fish." I'll have the rabbit ready in a bit."

I took the fish in the back door to the kitchen where mama was just pulling a pan of fresh biscuits out of the oven. She looked up at me as the screen door slammed.

"Y'all are back early," she said with a questioning look on her face.

"We are", I said. "There was a bear in the woods."

Mom gave me a concerned look. It's a bit early in the day for the bears to be roaming around.

"I thought so too", I told her. "But Dad said there was a rogue bear".

For just a split second mom got a strange look on her face. She turned to put the hot pan on the counter. "Then it's best you kids don't play near the woods today", she said.

I sat the bucket of fish on the counter beside the sink and went back out to get the rabbit. As I rounded the barn I could see dad down at the far end of the yard setting the bucket on the stump. I had often wondered what kind of animals showed up to eat. Rain and I had sat for hours watching that bucket, but we never saw any animals.

I guess they came at night while we were all asleep. Maybe I could talk her into sitting up with me one night and we could watch the animals as they showed up to eat.

I walked across the yard and joined dad at the edge of the woods. "Do you think the bear will come"? I asked.

"Don't know". "But I want you and your sister to stay away from the woods for the next few days." "You hear me"? Dad asked, giving me a stern look.

"Yes sir", I replied. "Rain and I will play up near the house or in the barn."

"Good girl". Dad put his arm across my shoulders and led me back across the yard. "Let's get this rabbit in the house for your mom. I'm looking forward to some dumplings tonight."

Chapter two

I did talk Rain into sitting out with me, but it was a few years later. I was about thirteen and Rain would have been twelve. We had planned to slip out of the house around midnight. Our dad usually went to bed after the nightly news and I would always hear him climbing the stairs to his and mom's bedroom. It wouldn't be but a few minutes and he would be snoring loudly, this would be my cue to slip out of my room and go wake up Rain.

I lay there in my warm bed contemplating the fact that my bed was warm and I knew it would be freezing outside. It crossed my mind to just forget about our plan as I pulled the blanket up under my chin. But I was curious about the animals.

I reluctantly pulled the cover back and climbed out of bed. The cold air hit me instantly. Dad kept the fire roaring all night, but it never seemed to warm the upper floor. Mom had finally talked him into getting electric heat installed, but he kept the thermostat set so low that it hardly ever came on.

I pulled my jeans on over my pajama bottoms Stepped into my boots and grabbed my heavy coat.

I slowly eased my bedroom door open and heard dad's snoring become louder. He was fast asleep. I knew if he woke up and found Rain and I gone, we would be in terrible trouble. But this was a chance we were going to have to take.

I tiptoed out into the hall as quietly as I could and made my way to Rain's room, avoiding every board that I knew would creak or groan.

Rain's room was just at the top of the stairs so I was a few feet further away from mom and dad's room now. The moonlight shining through the windows gave enough light for me to make out her small form on the bed bundled under the covers. As I entered the room, I could hear the gentle snores.

"Rain"! I whispered, as loudly as I dared. She didn't move at all. I crept closer to the bed. "Rain"! I whispered again. This time, the figure beneath the blankets stirred slightly.

"Come on Rain", I urged. "Dads went to bed".

She gave an inaudible groan and turned over. I reach out and shook her arm. "Come on, let's go watch the animals".

Rain stirred slightly under the covers. She stretched and then slowly set up.

I grabbed her jeans and handed them to her.

"It's so cold," she said; reaching for her pants.

" I know", I said. "But don't you want to know what comes and eats from the bucket"?

"I guess so", she said pulling on her coat.

We quietly slipped out of the room and down the stairs. I made my way through the dark kitchen by the slight glimmer of the moon shining through the windows. Tonight was a full moon. It should give us plenty of light to see across the yard. As I opened the kitchen door the winter air surrounded me instantly. I mentally kicked myself for not planning this for the summer. I just assumed that there would be more animals taking advantage of a free meal in the winter than there would be in the summer months.

Rain and I crept across the back yard. There was no sound other than the crunching of our feet on the frozen ground. We were heading to the back side of the barn. If we sat there we would have a full view of the tree line.

I had picked us a good spot earlier in the day and moved a few of dad's things so we could sit down and lean against the wall.

Rain started around the side of the barn, but I grabbed her arm and motioned for her to follow me. I wanted to go through the barn and grab a horse blanket. It was freezing cold out here.

We entered the barn and was greeted with the smell of horses and straw. Dad had cut the fresh hay last Summer and it was still giving off its heavy smell. I didn't want to walk through the barn and get the horses stirred up, so I had moved one of the blankets earlier in the day. It was still hanging on a nail at the first stall, just where I had left it. I grabbed the blanket and headed back for the front door.

"Why don't we just go out the back door"? Rain asked.

"Because I don't want to upset the horses and opening the back door of the barn may spook any animals that have come up to eat", I whispered.

Rain shrugged her shoulders and followed me.

She and I made our way quietly around the barn and took our seats beside dad's work table. There was plenty of moonlight for us to see across the yard. If anything came out of the tree line, we would have a good view of it.

We covered up with the horse blanket and settled in to wait. It wasn't long before I saw a raccoon come slowly out of the woods. He sniffed around a little and then disappeared back into the shadows. I wondered why he hadn't approached the bucket. Raccoon's loved to eat fish. Could it already be empty? I sat there with my eyes glued to the old stump. It wasn't long before I thought I saw another shadow just at the edge of the yard. I rubbed my eyes and looked again. This shadow looked like a man. But it was still in the darkness so I couldn't be sure.

"Rain, do you see that"? I whispered
"Rain"? I whispered again a bit more urgently. I looked over to see why she hadn't answered me and this is when I realized that she was sound asleep. I nudged her with my arm.

"Rain, look", I said pointing to the tall shadow.

I felt her sit up higher so she could see what I was pointing at.

"That's a man," she gasped. "What is he doing in our yard"?

" I don't know" I whispered back. "Let's see what he does."

We sat there watching as this shadow moved back and forth just inside the tree line. It was like he knew that we were there and wouldn't come completely out in the open. I was a little frightened to know that there was a strange man on our property in the middle of the night. I just knew this had to be the man that was stealing our animals. We had random chickens goats and pigs go missing from time to time with no sign of who took them.

I had considered going back to the safety of the house. But the spot I had chosen for our animal watch was not well hidden. If Rain and I stood up now, this stranger would have a full view of us. Just the thought of this made my heart skip a beat. We had no choice but to sit here until the man left.

I noticed a horrible smell being carried up across the yard. Was that the bucket? Surely it couldn't smell that bad this quickly. This smelled like something rotten.

"Why is he just pacing back and forth like that"? Rain asked. "Can he see us"?

"I don't think he can as long as we don't move," I whispered back.

I was beginning to wonder if coming out here had been such a good idea after all. What if this man had come to steal animals and found us here hiding? Would he kill us? Would he kidnap us? I was so frightened that I wanted to cry. Would mom and dad even hear us if we started screaming?

It wasn't long before I heard something. I sat up and strained my ears toward the woods. I was almost certain that I had heard a bear huffing. I didn't want to alarm Rain so I sat perfectly still trying to hear.

As I listened, there was a strange yell that came from further in the woods. I had never heard anything like this! It sounded like a mix between a coyote and a Mountain Lion. I had no idea what animal would make this noise.

Rain grabbed a hold of my arm tightly. "What was that "? she asked with her voice shaking. I could tell she was about ready to cry. As frightened as I was this had to be really scary for her.

" I think that was a mountain Lion", I told her. Knowing full well that it wasn't. "It is probably just over the next ridge and its voice carried up the hollow".

"That scared me to death"! She said. Not letting go of my arm.

I noticed that the man had stopped pacing back and forth and was now standing completely still. It looked like there was a shorter person with him now. I wished I could see better. But the moon wasn't strong enough to penetrate the woods.

"Do you see two people now"? Rain whispered.

"Yes", I responded. "Maybe they will leave soon". The fact that there appeared to be two people now really had my nerves on edge. I was certain these men were thieves. I knew I had to find a way to get myself and my sister back inside the house. Something just didn't feel right. It felt dangerous to be out here.

"I wish we had a dog", Rain said.

"What"? I asked.

"I wish we had a dog. It would run barking at these men and scare them away", she said.

I had never thought about that, but she did have a good idea. I would talk to mom and dad about that tomorrow. I leaned back against the wall and watched for any movement in the woods. Either my eyes had grown tired from straining them or the men had left. I wasn't seeing any shadows where they had been earlier. Should Rain and I make a run for the house now, or should we wait a little longer and make sure that they were truly gone and not just hiding?

"I don't see them anymore," said Rain, as if she had been reading my mind.

"I know", I replied. "Let's sit here just a minute and make sure they are gone".

After a little while, I still wasn't seeing any movement so I whispered to Rain. "I am going to count to three when I say three I want you to get on your hands and knees keeping your head down and crawl behind me. We will go along the side of the barn where it's darkest until we reach the front. Then we will stand up and run for the kitchen door, I said.

Be as quiet as you can and whatever you do, don't scream"!

"OK", Rain said.

"One...Two...Three! I whispered as loudly as I dared. Rain and I were up on our knees and crawling as fast as we could for the side of the barn. The frozen ground was stinging my palms. We reach the side of the barn and crawled as fast as we could down the length of it. I had never realized just how big this barn was! I was beginning to get tired and my knees were hurting, but I didn't dare stand up. We finally turned the corner to the front of the barn and I leaped to my feet planting my back against the wall. Once we left the barn and headed for the house we would be out in the open. If there was anyone in the woods, they would surely see us then. But I didn't think they could run fast enough to get us before we reach the back door. Unless they had a gun. I mentally scolded myself for that thought.

" I'm going to count to three again, I told her. On three, I want you to run as fast and as quietly as you can for the kitchen door. Once we get to the door, stop. And let me open the door easy, so mom and dad don't hear us".

"Uh huh" rain nodded. I could tell she was scared to death and so was I. I didn't know what would happen once we were out in the open running. But I had to get us both back into the house.

"One...Two...Three"!

I grabbed her arm and ran as fast as I could for the back door. I hadn't considered the fact that Rain's legs were shorter than mine and she fell about half way across the yard. She went down hard and slid across the frozen ground. She had already begun to cry as I helped her to her feet.

"I skinned my palms", she said, holding her hands out. I was scared to death to be standing here in the open! My heart was pounding and my stomach was in knots. I could feel something watching us and It felt like it was going to charge us at any minute.

"We have got to get in the house"! I whispered loudly. "Come on"! I grabbed her by the arm and tried to drag her toward the house.

Just then I heard a scream that I have never heard before. It was deep and loud. It vibrated through my chest like a base drum at a Christmas parade! I felt the repercussion as much as I heard it. Rain and I both froze. I was frozen in place. I couldn't speak. I couldn't run. I just stood there frozen with a fear that I had never known. It was the creature from the woods! There really was a monster in the woods!

This scream had come from the lower part of the yard where we had seen the two men earlier. There was something down there!

'Raven, What was that"? Rain asked with panic in her voice.

"Come on"! I grabbed her arm again and ran for the house. This time, I didn't care if she fell or not I would just drag her the rest of the way If I had to. Something was out here with us and we had to get inside!

My heart was still pounding as I gently closed the front door and slid the bolt. Everything in me wanted to slam the door fast so nothing could get in! We were safe now.

I took a deep breath and let it out slowly trying to calm the pounding of my heart. I eased over to the kitchen window and looked down to the lower part of the yard. There was nothing out there. Just moonlight creating a thousand diamonds on the frozen grass. Whatever had made that noise was gone now.

But what was it? Could a Mountain Lion scream like that? The creature that made that noise was much bigger than any mountain lion. And the scream had been deep and guttural, almost like a growl. It would have to have been something huge. The biggest thing we had in our area was a black bear and I had never heard a bear make a scream like that. I had felt it in my chest. I had felt the vibration of the scream. I thought about asking dad about it tomorrow but then I would have to tell him what we did. There was no way I could mention this to him.

And I didn't think Rain and I would be going outside to watch the animals in the middle of the night again anytime soon. But as I had this thought I felt the slightest flicker of curiosity inside. As frightened as I was, something deep inside was curious as to what animal had made this sound.

Naturally, I didn't mention this to my parents. I knew there would be a very harsh punishment if they found out I had drug my little sister outside with me in the middle of the night. And right now, I was regretting that decision. Something had been out there with us and I could have gotten us killed.

"We need to go get back in our beds now, before we wake mom and dad ", I whispered to her. I was still frightened. And I felt like something was watching us. I knew I wouldn't be sleeping tonight.

" Can I please sleep in your room"? She asked. I could hear the tears in her voice.

" OK", I told her. "But if mom or dad ask, just tell them you had a bad dream".

" I promise", she said with a big smile.

We made our way quietly up the stairs to my bedroom.

Chapter 3

Time went by and the night of watching the bucket had been pushed to the back of my mind. Rain and I had gotten older, now twelve and eleven, and we were both able to help out more around the house. Growing up the way we did, it seemed like the chores were endless. But mom and dad allowed us plenty of free time to just be kids.

Early on Summer mornings, while the air was still cool. Rain and I would have to water the garden, pull the weeds and pick whatever vegetable was ready. We carried plastic laundry baskets to put the ripened vegetables in, the rotten ones were thrown into a buckets for the pigs and the wildlife. Once we had our basket full we would carry it around to the outside spigot and wash the dirt off. Then we would set the full basket on the back porch pick up an empty basket from the stack and do it all over again. This usually took us until late morning. Then we could go play until supper time. After supper, we would pick the fruit from the fruit trees. Mom always insisted the fruit be picked in the evenings.

This particular summer had been harder than usual. We had been suffering from a bad drought. The well water we had been using in the garden was almost gone.

Once it ran out we would be forced to haul water all the way from the river. Using city water would just cost too much. That was only used in the house.

I had gone out this morning before Rain. I wanted to get finished with our chores early today and meet some local kids at the river. I knew mom and dad wouldn't mind as long as our chores were through.

I grabbed a basket off the back porch and headed out to the garden. I loved the coolness of the morning. But I knew just as soon as the sun topped the mountain the coolness would be replaced with an unrelenting heat.

I set my basket down on the grass at the head of the garden. I had planned to weed and pick the eggplant as I went then all I would have to do is come back to water them. I weeded the first plant. There were small eggplants, but none big enough to be picked. The next few plants were the same way. I raised my head to look down the row I was working on. I gasped! There wasn't an eggplant in sight! The garden had been full of them yesterday. Then it dawned on me. I bet dad picked them last night and in my hurry to get started, I didn't pay attention to them sitting on the back porch. I better go make sure they had been washed and would be ready for mama this morning.

I walked around the house to the back porch. There were no full baskets there. Just the empty baskets ready to be filled this morning. This just didn't make any sense. What happened to the Eggplant? I stood there for a moment pondering the missing vegetable. Then I remembered that I wanted to get done early today so I hurried back to the garden.

I picked up my basket and moved one row over to the squash. At least, the squash was still here. I had worked about half of the row weeding and picking when the same thing began to happen again. I would come across four or five plants with no squash. I moved the next plant aside to pull the weeds from underneath it and that's when I saw it. A huge bare footprint, half way hidden beneath the plant. I pulled the leaves back and looked closer. That was a really big footprint. It looked like the thieves may have come back. I bet they took the eggplant. I stepped over to the next row and sure enough, it was covered in these bare footprints! Most of them were really big but I did notice a few that were somewhat smaller. Still big enough, to be an adult, though. I looked down at my own feet, clad in riding boots. Mom and dad never let us work the garden barefoot. There was a good chance of a snake being hidden under the plants seeking shade from the hot sun.

I thought about telling dad about the prints. But decided to wait until after we went swimming. If he thought there was a thief roaming around, he may not let us go.

I finished up with the little bit of squash that was left. and moved on over to the peppers. There were the same prints here as well, just not as many. I guess our thief preferred eggplant and squash.

It was just after lunch when Rain and I had finished up with our chores. The garden had been picked, weeded and watered. We cleaned the horse stalls, fed the pigs and were just turning the goats out to pasture. We were both excited to be going swimming. I fastened the gate on the goat pen and we raced for the house.

We grabbed clean towels from the clothesline and raced to the trail-head, while mom yelled from the back porch. "You girls be back before it gets dark, and Raven, watch your sister"!

We slowed down to a walk as we entered the trail. The temperature was noticeably cooler here with the thick tree coverage. The sun on the pine trees had caused them to release their heavy scent, creating a pleasant Summer time aroma.

I pondered telling Rain about the footprints I found in the garden this morning. I wouldn't have to worry about her keeping a secret now.

I was going to tell dad at dinner tonight. He needed to know that the thief was still roaming around. But I didn't want him to get worried, and spoil our swimming fun. I knew he would have told us to stay home.

As we got to the fork in the trail Rain and I veered right. We would be going down to the falls today. That is where we usually met up with our friends. It was fun to stand underneath the falls and let the water run over you. And the falls emptied out into a small lake before narrowing back into the river. This was the perfect place for swimming.

As we neared the falls I noticed right away that the rush of the water was quieter today. The falls weren't as loud as they usually were. I didn't hear any laughing or squealing either. Normally, by now we could hear the sounds of the kids playing in the water.

"It sure is quiet", Rain said.

"Maybe they are just taking a break from swimming", I replied.

We rounded the bend and stepped out into the clearing. We were shocked to find that there was no one there. But it didn't take long to realize why. The drought had caused the water to recede and become extremely muddy. Even the water coming off the falls had an orange tint to it.

'Eeew" commented Rain.

Eeew was right. There was no way we could swim in this water.

" I bet everyone's at the pool", I said with a sigh.

"I don't want to go to the city pool" Rain whined.

"We couldn't even if we wanted to," I said. "Mom is too busy to take us and Dad is over helping Uncle Luke."

"What do we do now"? She asked.

"Let's walk on up the river", I said. Maybe we can find a spot that isn't so bad. If we go back now we will have to help mom in the kitchen.

"Let's go!" She said with a smile.

As we walked along the river I was shocked to see just how muddy it had become. The water that was once crystal clear now had a muddy orange tint to it.

We stopped at our fishing spot and walked down to the edge of the water. It was well beyond what had once been the bank. I couldn't ever remember seeing the water this low. It was beginning to concern me. What if it dried up? What if we ran out of water altogether? Would we die? I scolded myself for having such silly thoughts.

I looked across the now shrinking river and saw the bank with the Mountain Laurel. Maybe today would be a good day to go exploring.

" Come on", I said to Rain as I started across the river.

"Where are we going"? She asked with a puzzled look on her face.

"We've never been to this side," I called, looking back at her over my shoulder.

 I pulled off my boots and walked out into the water. It looked shallow enough for us to walk across without much problem. But if the water got too deep it would be OK. Rain and I both were good swimmers.

"Wait for me," Rain whined from the bank.

"Just come on," I said, getting a little annoyed with her. She and I were really very close. But she was younger and still had moments of being a cry baby.

The water was now up to my waist, but it wasn't rushing like it normally did so I was still able to walk without any problem. I made it to the far bank and turned to see where Rain was. She was about to the middle of the river now holding her boots and towel above her head just as I had.

"You're doing great", I told her. "Just a little farther."

I waited until she reach the bank with me then I turned to look at the thick forest behind us.

"Let's go look around," I said, ducking under the branches. They were so low I had to walk hunched over. It was much cooler inside the trees. We hadn't gone far when the trees gave way to a small clearing. I straightened up and looked around. The tall grass had been mashed down here. I bet it was where the deer had been bedding as they passed through. It was a nice hidden spot for them to rest and the tree canopy provided them ample shade.

"I like it here", Rain said. Walking into the middle of the clearing and laying down on her back.

I looked around at the small clearing and thought about a club house. I could picture myself lying on this soft grass and reading on Summer afternoons.

"Why don't we make this our clubhouse," I suggested.

"Yes!" exclaimed Rain eagerly. "That would be fun. And It will be just ours. We won't let anyone else in".

"Let's go see what we can find to use", I said, ducking under the branches.

It was much cooler here and it would be the perfect place for a clubhouse. 'We can get some cattails to put down to lay on", I said. "And we can get some river rocks to make a pretend fireplace"

"I can get some cedar branches", Rain said excitedly. "We can use them to sit on"!

For the next hour or two Rain and I busied ourselves with building our little house in the woods.

I brought the last load of cattails into the clearing and dropped them. I was hot, sweaty and tired. I lay down on the soft grass and it immediately felt good on my tired muscles. Rain plopped down beside me and we lay there looking up at the branches to the blue sky peeking through here and there.

'This is nice", Rain said."I could just stay right here forever".

"uh huh," I responded. I could already feel my eyes getting heavy. A short nap wouldn't hurt.

I woke suddenly to something hitting me in my chest. I sat up and looked around. I was confused as to where I was to start with. I wasn't familiar with my surroundings. The sun had moved further across the sky creating shadows on the ground. Rain was still asleep on the grass beside me. What had woken me up? I looked down beside my leg to see a small river rock. Had this hit me? Where would a rock have come from? Who would have thrown it? I was looking around the tree line to see if anyone was playing a joke when another rock came from behind me and hit me in the back! This one had been more forceful than the last and sort of hurt. I quickly looked over my shoulder, but I still couldn't see anything. As I was looking behind me, I heard Rain blurt out,

'Stop it Raven"! "That hurts"!

She too was now sitting up looking sleepy and confused.

"I didn't do it", I exclaimed. "Someone is throwing rocks at us."

We were being hit by rocks, but I couldn't tell where they were coming from. It seemed like they were coming from every direction all at the same time, but how?

"Come on", I said. "Let's go home." I stood up to gather my things and heard the strangest bird I have ever heard. "Whoop!" Then another answered from behind us, "whoop!" I got a horrible feeling in the pit of my stomach. That wasn't a bird. I was sure of it.

"Come on!" Hurry up"! I yelled.

Rain and I made a mad dash for the trees that would lead us back to the river. I knew it would be slow going to get through the underbrush, but we hurried as fast as we could. Just as we broke the tree line at the river another rock landed on the ground beside me rolling down toward the water.

My heart was pounding in my ears and I was more frightened than I had ever been! Something about this just didn't feel right. I wanted out of these woods with everything in me. But home was a long way off just yet.

I crossed the water as quickly as I could and was making my way up the bank when I heard Rain yell, "Raven!" 'Slow Down!"

I looked back to see where she was and I saw what appeared to be a very large, black, monkey duck behind a large oak tree!

"Run Rain!, I screamed.

Chapter 4

Rain and I made it back safely to the house that day and I never told anyone about what I saw. Who would have believed me anyway? After some time went by I even began telling myself that I had been mistaken. It had to have been a trick of the shadows.

Rain asked on occasion why we didn't go back to our clubhouse. I just told her that it wasn't private anymore since someone had been there throwing rocks at us. I told her we would find another place soon. But I knew I had no intention of doing that again. There was something or someone out there and it didn't want us around.

The drought finally made our fishing become difficult. There just wasn't that many fish with the water receding the way it was. When dad and I went now we could spend all morning fishing and maybe leave with five. I had never seen it like this. And the worried look on my dads face made me, even more, worried.

Our garden was beginning to dry up because it was just too difficult to carry that much water up from the river. We tried to do the best we could, but each day we were losing more and more of the garden.

Lately, after Dad cleaned the fish he would have me throw some of our sun dried vegetables in the bucket too. I guess he figured if we couldn't eat them, the animals could. And like it always had been, dad would carry the bucket down to the old stump at the edge of the yard.

I had forgotten all about the footprints I had found until one day I went to take some of the dead vegetable plants out to the pig pen. I was pouring my bucket into their food trough when I saw another one of those bare footprints near the fence. It looked like someone had just stepped right over the fence! But what man would be tall enough to do that? It just wasn't possible. I was pondering this as the pigs rooted around in the trough making grunting noises over their food. Hearing dad's truck coming up the long driveway, stopped my train of thought.

" Come look what I have"! He yelled, slamming the truck door. I hurried out of the pen closing and latching the door behind me and ran for the truck. Rain, hearing dad's voice came running from the house. We reach the truck just in time to see dad lifting a young pup over the side! A dog! Dad had gotten us a dog! I immediately went down on my knees and was greeted with a wet tongue and tail wags.

He was just beautiful! As I wrapped my arms around him dad lifted yet another dog out of the truck! 'And I guess this would be his brother', he said, sitting the pup on the ground in front of Rain. Two dogs!

"Where did you get them"? I asked, laughing at the pup trying to lick my face as I talked.

"They were on the side of the road," dad replied. "I got out and called for their mom but they seemed to be the only two there. I couldn't just leave them to fend for themselves. Pups this young would never be able to fight off the coyotes".

The screen door slammed as mom came out onto the front porch wiping her hands on a dish towel. "What is all the fuss going on out here?" she asked.

"We have puppies"! Rain exclaimed.

"What in the world..mom thought aloud as she walked out to the truck. She walked up to dad and he draped his arm across her shoulders.

"They were abandoned on the side of the road" I explained.

Mom looked down at the two pups that were happily attacking Rain and me with kisses. "They are a cute pair," she said. "What kind of dogs are they?"

" I'm thinking, a shepherd mix, as far as I can tell" dad answered. "At least they will make good watch dogs and maybe the chickens and livestock will stop going missing'" he added.

"I'm all for that," mom said, heading back to the house. "Dinner will be done shortly. Then I need you girls to take care of the cherry and crab apple trees", mom added.

'We will"! Rain and I answered in unison.

Dad stood there for a while, watching Rain and I play with the new puppies. "I guess we need to go get them a place fixed in the barn", he finally said.

"The barn"? Rain asked. "Why can't they stay in the house"?

"Well, they won't be much help running off the thieves if they are sleeping all snug inside", dad said with a laugh. "Bring them on and we'll fix them a good spot".

We got the pups settled into the barn where we knew they would be safe until they got a little bigger. Dad told us how we would need to care for them and showed us how to brush out their coats and check their nails for any splits. I was so excited to have my very own dog! I was already tossing names around in my head. I would have to find the perfect name for him.

We spent the rest of that Summer doing our chores with Max and Jackson following us everywhere we went. Being brothers, they looked a lot alike. But their attitudes were very different.

Max was Rains and he barked at everything. Dad would often get upset with the noise he would cause during the night. Jackson was my dog and he was very laid back. He hardly ever barked. If he did, you could be sure that he saw something. It could be nothing more than a fox or a raccoon, but he would let you know it was there. And then he was going to chase it away.

It was late Summer now but still plenty hot enough for Rain and me to enjoy the river. We had gotten some recent rains that seemed to help with the fishing but it just wasn't enough to bring the river back up to where it should be. Dad said it could sometimes take a few years to recover from such a harsh drought.

It was a beautiful Saturday morning and dad asked us to exercise the horses after we finished our chores. This usually meant riding them around the pasture. We could exercise the horses and check the fence lines for dad at the same time. I was really disappointed because I had wanted to go to the river and pick Blueberries. But now that we had to ride the horses, I wouldn't get to. It usually took us, at least, two hours to exercise the horses and that wouldn't leave us enough time to get up to the river and pick berries before dark.. I was feeling angry with dad for finding us more work to do when it occurred to me, that we could just take the berry buckets and look for berries as we exercised the horses.

After lunch Rain and I ran for the barn. We grabbed the buckets, saddled our horses and headed out with Max and Jackson following. The day was beautiful and I was feeling good so it didn't take long for Rain and me to have our horses at a nice gallop going along the fence. I wasn't really paying attention to the fence like I should have been. I was looking at the tree line for berry bushes. With the Summer beginning to fade, there weren't as many bushes left with berries on them. The animals had already gotten to most of them. After riding for about half an hour, I spotted some bushes that still looked to be pretty full. I couldn't believe my luck!

These bushes looked like they hadn't been touched all season! And had been spared by the drought. It didn't occur to me to question why there was such a beautiful stand of blueberries here. It was almost as if someone had tended them.

We tethered the horses to the fence and climbed over with our buckets.

We didn't have to enter the woods to begin picking. The large full bushes were spilling out between the trees. But naturally as we picked we moved further and further into the woods without even realizing it. After a while, I looked up to see Rain shove a handful of the big ripe berries in her mouth.

"How are we supposed to fill our buckets when you're eating them like that"? I asked "Wouldn't you rather eat them in mom's pie'?

She smiled real big showing me her now blue teeth. "I can eat as many as I want". She thumped a berry at me striking me in the chest. A full blown battle ensued! We were laughing and throwing berries at each other. I am sure the sounds of our squealing could be heard all the way down the mountain.

I was just about to throw a handful of berries when I heard the deep splintering sound of a large tree cracking just before it falls. We stopped, holding our breath and waiting for the earth shattering thud of the tree hitting the ground. The sound never came. Nothing but eerie silence followed. This just didn't feel right. All of a sudden A strong sense of fear washed over my entire body.

We both froze in place listening to the sound of the forest. It was like waiting for thunder after the lightning has struck. You know something is supposed to follow and when it doesn't there is a certain eeriness that fills the air. Breaking the silence, there was an ear-splitting sound of branches breaking and trees being shoved over! I swear it sounded like a large freight train was coming right for us! The sound of the chaos coming through the woods caused my heart to race and my blood went cold. Rain and I turned and ran for the fence! Something big was coming through those woods and we were terrified!

We climbed the fence just as Jackson scooted under it. He was heading for whatever was making that noise while barking and growling! I yelled for him as I mounted my horse. He hesitated for only a minute before he turned with a whimper and ran past us heading back for the house with Max close to his heels.

This caused my fear to increase ten-fold. I had never seen this dog scared of anything! We didn't waste any time doing the same thing. I kept spurring my horse on until we were at a full run! I looked over my shoulder to see Rain right behind me. Good! I felt a wave of relief knowing that's Rain's horse could keep up and I knew Rain was a good enough rider to keep herself in the saddle. I risked a glance back at the woods we had just left and I saw something big step back into the shadows. As if it were standing there watching us. It was only for a split second as I didn't dare lose my grip on the horse. But my stomach felt sick just seeing this shadow. I had a horrible feeling of impending doom.

We got home and brought our horses into the barn. Jackson and Max were nowhere to be seen. I assumed they had run to the house.

Rain and I brushed down our horses without even talking. I think we were both in shock. There was no explanation for what happened. It all kept running through my mind over and over. What was that? What broke the tree? What could be big enough to cause that kind of noise? What did I see step back into the shadows? Were the stories about Kecleh-Kudleh really true?

'Raven", What was that back there"? Rain asked, as if reading my mind. "What caused that tree to come down"?

" I don't know", I told her. "Something strange is going on."

"I know", she said softly, "and it scares me."

" I don't think there's any reason to be frightened", I told her. " We just need to pay more attention when we're out in the woods." I wasn't about to tell her that I was scared to death. I was her older sister, and it was my job to make her feel better.

"Don't tell mom or dad that we left the berry buckets", I said. "We can go back for them tomorrow".

"I'm not going back there!" Rain said adamantly. That was the Kecleh-Kudleh!

I spun around to look at her. "How do you know that was the Kecleh-Kudleh"?

" Because it follows us", Rain said, dropping her head.

"What do you mean, "It follows us," I questioned.

"Tell me what you know." I took a step toward her. I looked around to make sure no one could hear us.

" I don't know for positive", she said. "But something has been knocking on my window at night. And then when you and I go out alone lately, something happens to scare us."

I felt a sense of relief. "There is no way anything is knocking on your window", I said. "Your window is on the second floor and much too high for anything to reach". I bet it's a squirrel or a bird", I told her.

" I don't know", she said doubtfully.

" Of course, it is", I told her. You're just letting things get to you. I'm sure there is an explanation for everything that has happened."

I could see that this had made her feel better. But I had every intention of asking dad about the Kecleh-Kudleh tonight.

That night after helping mom clean up from dinner, Rain went to watch TV, so I headed out to the front porch where dad was.

He was sitting in his rocker enjoying his pipe before we watched TV. I sat down in the chair next to him. We sat for a few minutes listening to the crickets and frogs with neither of us speaking.

"What's on your mind", dad finally asked.

"Have you ever seen the Kecleh-Kudleh"? I asked, looking over at him as I sat down.

"Now, what in the world made you ask that"? He said.

" I don't know", I replied. "People at school say they have seen it, and I was wondering if you have."

Dad inhaled from his pipe and let it out slowly. He was looking out across the yard as if he was lost in thought."

After a bit, he began to speak. "Stories of the Kecleh-Kudleh have been around as long as these mountains have." It is part of our heritage as much as the land itself. Of course, people are going to claim to have had encounters with them". He drew threw his pipe again and I waited for him to continue. " I don't know that there is anything out there. But I don't find it a good idea to take any chances."

He continued to look out across the yard. I was growing impatient waiting on him to answer my question. So I finally asked again, 'Have you ever seen one?"

Dad took a deep breath, and let it out with a sigh. He didn't want to answer me! He had seen one! I was sure of it in the way he was being so hesitant!

" I have seen things I can't explain," he said. And some things are best not talked about". He stood up from his chair and walked over to the steps. He bent down and tapped his pipe out on the side of the porch. " You and your sister were raised here on this mountain", he said. "You have been taught to respect the land and our heritage." "You have been taught to be cautious and pay attention to the woods. You have the skills to handle yourself pretty well. You and your sister have nothing to fear." Now, he said." Enough talk, let's go watch some TV". He walked over to the door and opened it for me.

I didn't watch much TV that night. All of what dad had said was going over and over in my mind. He hadn't come right out and confirmed seeing anything. But, he hadn't told me no, either. For me, all that did was raise more questions and only add to my confusion.

Chapter 5

The years passed slowly and things around our farm had stayed pretty much the same. My sister and I grew older, fourteen and fifteen. And just like dad had said, we suffered from the drought for a few years to come. The river level never did get back to where it once had been. Not until long after I was an adult.

Rain, even though she was fourteen now had taken to sleeping in my room the past few years. She was still being woken up by something tapping on her window at night. I tried on a few occasions to find out what it was, but even my flashlight revealed nothing. The only thing that let me know she was telling the truth was the single bare footprint just below her bedroom window. I questioned dad about this. And even showed him the print. He said it was either a bear or a thief. Either way, we were made to stay close by for the next few weeks.

As I grew older I learned more and more about Kecleh-Kudleh, or Bigfoot, or Sasquatch. I read everything I could get my hands on. I spent some time asking my older relatives, but that just got me hushed up pretty fast. Luckily, my mom, being raised in a different tribe was able to explain this to me.

My grandmother on my fathers side had come for a visit. After dinner, that evening she and my parents had gone outside while dad smoked his pipe. I loved hearing them talk about the "old days", so I went out to the front steps and sat down to listen.

Grandmother was asking dad if he would come by and check her fence, she said she had a few goats that had gotten out and gone missing. She was just too old and frail to walk the woods looking for them.

I turned to look at her, "Grandma, do you think it's the Kecleh-Kudleh"?

Everyone went silent as my grandmother gasped. She pointed one long skinny finger at me, and in a stern voice she said," Don't you ever say those words out loud! Never! Do you hear me"? And with that, she got up from her rocker and as quickly as she could went inside. I was shocked! My grandmother had always been one of the sweetest women I knew. My heart was broken, not only for the fact that I had upset her, but also the fact that she had spoken to me so harshly.

'It's OK Raven", my mom said. Patting my shoulder as she followed Grandmother inside.

The tears had started down my cheeks. "I'm going to the barn", I said, standing up and heading down the steps.

"Only for a few minutes," dad said. "It's getting late".

I sat in the barn and waited, hoping my grandmother would be in bed by the time I went back in.

Mom was sitting at the kitchen table with a cup of coffee as I came in the back door. She stood up and poured me a cup of warm cider. "Sit with me a minute", she said. Taking her seat back at the table.

"Is grandmother OK", I asked her.

Mom gave a little snort, "she is just fine. Your grandmother is just old and set in the ways of the ancestors. Sometimes she doesn't think before she speaks. I'm sure she doesn't mean any harm, but that's just the way she is. I know you didn't mean to upset her. And she knows it too. That's what I want to talk to you about", she said.

She took a sip from her cup and began."You mentioned the Kecleh-Kudleh to your grandmother. I know and your dad knows that you didn't mean any harm. But to your grandmother, that was one of the worst things that could happen".

"Why"? I asked.

Mom took another sip and let out a sigh before she began again. " As you know, Dads tribe believes the Kecleh-Kudleh to be the forest guardians. They believe that they can control the trapping and fishing. If you have found favor with the Kecleh-Kudleh then you will have a good season. Whether it be lots of game killed or lots of fish caught. But to upset the Kecleh-Kudleh is one of the worst things that can happen. They believe that once upset, Kecleh-Kudleh will not find favor with you again until the snow has covered the ground three times".

 I was fascinated by what she was telling me. Of course, the kids at school had told me pieces and parts of things they had overheard their parents saying. But you never knew if it was the truth or not. Most of the families had lost the earlier customs and they were slowly being replaced with more modern versions. So to hear my mom speak about this legend was a dream come true for me.

Mom sipped her coffee again and looked out the kitchen window. It was too dark outside to see anything but our own reflections, but still she stared as if lost in a far away place.

I cleared my throat and took a sip of my cider hoping it would bring her back to her train of thought and she would finish telling me about the Kecleh-Kudleh.

After a while mom took another sip, then she slowly set her cup down and looked at me. "Now you know what I am telling you is all ancient legends of your daddies tribe, right"?

"Uh huh", I nodded. Barely able to contain my excitement.

"The elders of the council believe that if you anger the Kecleh-Kudleh. They will lose favor with you, and, can make you and your family suffer. To be punished by the Kecleh-Kudleh is one of the worst things that could ever happen. It is said that along with creating havoc with hunting and fishing, they will also take your animals, take your children or take you if they are angry enough."

I gasped! I had never heard any of this before!

Mom continued, "It is said that by speaking the name of the Kecleh-Kudleh around more than one other person will anger them greatly. When speaking of them in a group, they do not know what your intentions are and they fear being hunted by man. So that is one of the reasons your grandmother got so upset tonight."

Mom took another sip and looked back toward the window. I felt that she had more to say, but I didn't want to push her fearing that she would end the conversation. I sat quietly and allowed her time to gather her thoughts.

Finally, mom looked at me and said, 'Your grandmother believes they took your grandfather and that is why she is so adamant about holding firm to this ancient belief."

I gasped again! I knew that my grandfather was killed before I was born, but I had always been told it was a hunting accident. This was the first I had heard of anything like this. I was now terrified and fascinated!

"What really happened to grandpa"? I asked.

Mom let out a soft sigh, and said, "Raven the only reason I am telling you any of this is because I know your grandmother hurt you tonight and I feel that you are now owed an explanation. I can't give you that explanation without giving you the truth. The only thing I ask of you in return is to never tell any of this to your sister. I will speak with her too when the time is right.

Promise me that you will always respect the beliefs of your father's tribe and not ever mention the Kecleh-Kudleh again with more than one person. You are close enough to being an adult now so there is no need for taking any unwanted chances.

"I promise mama", I said. "And I am very sorry that I did it, but I didn't know"... I felt the tears welling up in my eyes and the sharp pain in my throat. I had scared my grandmother and I felt terrible about it. I wanted to find a way to make it right.

" I know that sweetie", mom said, reaching across the table to pat my hand. ' It's really my own fault for not telling you this sooner."

"But what happened to grandpa", I asked again.

Mom looked down at her coffee cup as if it was giving her the words to use. " Your grandfather didn't believe that the Kecleh-Kudleh actually existed. He had lived his whole life in these mountains hunting and trapping and it was his belief that if they existed he would have seen them. Like the rest of us, he had random animals go missing from time to time, but he always blamed it on bear and mountain lions along with a few rogue thieves. But to him, there was no such thing as the Kecleh-Kudleh.

One morning he had gone out to feed his livestock and he noticed that a part of the fence had been smashed down. He checked the animals and had two pigs and a goat missing.

As he was mending the fence your Uncle John had stopped by for a visit. He and your grandmother had walked out to where grandpa was working. They were all three standing there chatting in the field when Luke asked his father if he thought the Kecleh-Kudleh could have taken the animals. Being raised by your grandfather, John had no fear of them either because his own father told him they didn't exist. Your Grandmother reacted much the same way she had tonight. But your grandfather just laughed at her and said there was no such thing. He said it was probably a bear. Then, as if to mock them, he yelled toward the woods, 'If I ever see a hairy Kecleh-Kudleh stealing my animals I will take a shotgun to him!" Do you hear me Kecleh-Kudleh!?" Your grandmother was horrified and scared to death. She ran back to the house and wouldn't come out for days fearing what the Kecleh-Kudleh would do .

Later that day, your grandpa went out to check his traps and look for this bear he thought was stealing the animals. Grandma waited for him all of that evening, but he never returned home. When he still wasn't back by sunrise the next morning, she called her sons to go look for him.

She feared that he may have fallen or become sick and couldn't make it back to the house. Your dad, Luke, and John went out into the woods to look for him. They came across his hat first. It was hung on some bushes looking as if he had placed it there. And then they found one of his boots. It was laying on the ground underneath a tree. They crossed the river knowing that he had traps on the other side. At the first trap they came to, your Uncle John spotted grandpa's rifle about ten foot up in a tree. The barrel of the rifle had been completely bent in half. There was no blood anywhere and no other signs of your grandfather. It was like he had just disappeared. You father seems to think a bear got him and maybe he had used the gun to fight it off causing it to get bent.

'I sat there for a few minutes just staring at my mom. The Kecleh-Kudleh had taken my grandfather! My mind was reeling. It was going to take me some time to process all of this. I didn't want to speak for fear that I would interrupt anything else that she may want to tell me. I just sat there quietly wondering if there would be more.

Mom was still looking at the dark window when she said, "From the fear of what your grandfather had done was when your grandmother started offering the buckets of food.

She would take her left-overs from the house along with the remains of any animal she had cleaned and would put them in an old bucket and set it at the edge of her yard near the woods. She still does this today, Hoping they won't come for her if she continues to feed them", Mom turned to look at me when she finished speaking.

I was in shock. This was much more than I had ever expected and I wasn't sure what to do with all of this information. It was going to take me a while to dissect it all and let it sink in.

" Is that why dad does the bucket"? I asked.

" Yes", mom nodded. "He started that right after you were born ". I guess his reasoning is twofold. One, he wants to keep any possible Kecleh-Kudleh that may be out there, happy. And two, he feels if they are fed, like any other animal, they won't be as much of a danger".

" So he does this to keep us safe", I thought out-loud.

'Yes", Mom said. "Your father has never seen the Kecleh-Kudleh, so like me and you, he doesn't know for sure if they are out there or not. But it doesn't hurt anything to put the remains in a bucket just in case."

" But what happens if you have no food to offer them"? I asked.

"That is another story for another time", Mom said.

"Now","You know why your grandmother reacted the way she did tonight. And you know a few other things that I hope doesn't scare you. I would like you to keep this conversation just between me and you" she said. " I'm not sure how your dad and grandmother would d feel about my having told you all of this."

" I promise not to say anything," I told her.

'Good girl", mom said standing up and walking over to the sink. She rinsed out her cup and stood there a minute staring out the dark window. I was beginning to wonder if she actually could see anything besides her reflection looking back. There was something else she needed to say or something else she was keeping secret. But either way, I wanted to know what it was. I stood up and walked over to the sink with my own cup.

"Mama", I said softly.

She turned to look at me with the most honest eyes I have ever seen. She whispered so low it was barely audible, "yes", Yes Raven. Now, not another word, go to bed". Then she turned and left the kitchen. I don't know how long I stood there looking at the door she had just walked through. But it seemed like forever. She knew, She knew I was going to ask if she had ever seen one.

I wanted to go after her. I wanted to know what she had seen, but I knew she would never say anything more. Mom had told me all she was going to, and it was a lot for one night. I cut off the kitchen light and headed up the stairs to my bedroom. I had a lot to think about.

Chapter 6

The next morning I was still thinking about what mom had said as I was doing my chores. I was getting ready to rake out the horse stalls. I opened the stall and led my Meredith out the back door to the pasture. I didn't see the buckets sitting there on the ground. I went back in and passed Rain walking her Thunder out. I grabbed the rake and was just about to start when I hear Rain yell.

"Raven"! "Come here"! She called.

I propped up my rake and went to see what she wanted.

"What are you yelling about"? I asked as I walked out the door.

Rain was standing there holding her horses lead and pointing down at our two berry buckets. The ones we had left in the woods yesterday! "How did they get back here"? She asked quietly.

"Maybe mom or dad brought them back", I told her.

"Do you really thinks so"? She asked. "They didn't even know that we went berry picking".

I knew she was right. But I also didn't want to scare her any more than she already was. " Of course, I think so," I told her. "Buckets don't walk".

I picked them up and walked back into the barn. I took the buckets over to the wall and hung them up. How did they get here? If mom or dad had brought them back we would have been scolded for leaving them in the first place. And they would have been really angry that we went berry picking without telling them.

"Raven". I turned to see Rain standing behind me.
"I'm scared", she said.

" Why"? I asked. "There are a million ways those buckets could have been brought back", I told her. Knowing, that I was lying. I was just as scared as she was. Something or someone was out in those woods and it they were watching us. I had wondered if it were kids from school, but I quickly dropped that idea. They would have no way of knowing when Rain and I would be alone or when we would be out in the woods. This was something more than our friends. And it really scared me.

"I think the Kecleh-Kudleh are real. And I think they are here," she said quietly. My blood went cold just by hearing her say this.

" You shouldn't think that way just because of the buckets", I told her. "I'm sure someone saw them and brought them back."

" It's not just the buckets", she said. "I feel like they are after me", "Something looks in my windows at night. I can see it's eyes shining".

" You don't sleep in your room anymore", I reminded her. "You sleep in my room now. Or on the couch when you fall asleep early."

" They are looking in your window now". She said softly.

"You said you have only seen eyes", I reminded her. "That could be anything, a Raccoon, a opossum or even a Bobcat". Just because you saw some eyes doesn't mean it's the Kecleh-Kudleh", I told her.

She stood there with her head down as if studying the toe of her boot. "I know", she said. "I just feel like it is".

I realized at that moment that maybe I had been inadvertently scaring my younger sister. I had been the one focused on the Kecleh-Kudleh lately.

And it was starting to scare her. I told myself right then that I wouldn't think about this Kecleh-Kudleh anymore. And I would start keeping my little sister away from places that she might see as scary.

'You know what's funny"? I asked her.

"No", "What"? She asked, looking up at me.

" We have spent an awful lot of our Summer worrying about something that may not even exist", I said with a laugh.

"You're right", she said. That doesn't make us look very smart.

" No," "It doesn't", I said laughing. 'Now let's get our chores finished and have some fun".

" I never mentioned those buckets to mom and dad. I had made a promise to myself and my sister. I spent the rest of the summer trying to forget about the Kecleh-Kudleh.

The weather had begun to grow cooler, the leaves were changing and my sister and I were back in school. We got up early and took care of our horses and dogs before school.

Then our afternoons were filled with homework and helping mom in the kitchen. This was when a lot of the canning, baking and cooking were done to get ready for winter.

With the cooler weather, Rain and I had started sleeping with our windows open. I don't know what she had seen looking in at her over the Summer, but it seemed to be forgotten now.

Late one night I was woken up by the sounds of the horses and Max barking like crazy. Something had spooked them and they were having a fit. I got up to look out the window. There was an outside light now on the front side of the barn, but the doors were closed and I couldn't see anything.

Rain joined me at the window. She had her arms crossed across her chest shielding herself from the chilly air.
" What's going on"? She asked.

"Not sure", I responded. "The horses woke me up having a fit." Just then I saw Jackson run around to the back side of the barn barking like mad. Max could still be heard from the back side as well.

" Maybe I should go see," I said. Looking over at the twenty-two rifle propped in the corner. I had gotten it for my birthday and hadn't really had the chance to use it yet.

'Oh no you're not!" Rain said. "I'm going to wake dad. We have no clue what is out there," she was already leaving the room before I could respond.

I could hear their muffled voices coming from across the hall as Rain woke our parents.

I stood there watching out the window and wondering what had the animals so upset.

I heard Rain coming back across the hall and turned to look as she entered the bedroom. "Dad is going to check", she said.

When I turned back to the window, I saw something really big sprint from the barn into the woods. It went down across the yard and disappeared right behind the old stump. I let out a gasp without knowing.

" What"? Rain asked, rushing toward the window. "What did you see"?

" I think I saw a bear", I told her. I could feel her looking at me because she knew better. I wasn't about to tell her anything. I had made a promise not to scare her anymore and I had every intention of keeping it.

We both watched as dad left the front porch and walked toward the barn with his shotgun. The dogs were still barking and causing all kinds of noise. Dad opened the front barn door and disappeared inside.

In just a minute we heard a few gunshots and the dogs barking faded off into the woods. They were on the trail of what ever dad had just shot at. We heard dad whistle a few times for the dogs. He was calling them back. Then off in the distance we heard one of them screaming! The scream stopped as quickly as it started. Only one dog could be heard barking now! Rain and I looked at each other and raced from the bedroom! I could barely hold onto the banister as my feet flew down the stairs. I burst out the front door screaming, "Jackson!" Rain was right behind me screaming for Max.

We raced down the side of the barn with both of us still screaming at the top of our lungs. As I rounded the corner I almost plowed face first into the barn door!

I came to a quick stop and Rain ran into the back of me sending us both sprawling on the ground.

I looked up from my ground position and could see that the big barn door had been practically ripped from its hinges! The top hinge was the only thing left holding it up and the door had been bent straight out! The bear had ripped the barn door off to get in.

"Get back in the house"! Dad screamed at us. "Go now"! He yelled over his shoulder, as he jogged toward the woods with his gun. He was going after the dogs.

Rain and I scrambled to our feet and raced back toward the house. Both of us crying hysterically.

Mom had come out on the porch to see what was going on. She met us at the bottom of the steps wrapping us both in her arms. She must have heard dad yell at us because we were quickly pushed into the house where she closed the front door behind us.

" Are you both OK"? She asked urgently. Looking us both over quickly from head to toe.

Rain continued to cry uncontrollably.

'We're fine mom", I told her through my tears. "But one of the dogs is hurt bad. Dad went to check on him I think".

" It's going to be OK", mom said. 'If he's out there, your daddy will bring him back. Now let's go in the kitchen and have some warm cider while we wait". She put her arm around Rain and led her into the kitchen with me following.

It seemed like an eternity before we heard the front door open. We all three jumped up from our chairs as Jackson rounded the corner into the kitchen. I fell to my knees wrapping my arms around him as Rain and mom looked hopefully at the kitchen door. Dad stepped into the room with his head bowed down. He stood there for a few seconds and finally he looked up at Rain. "I couldn't find him", he said. Rain sank back down into her chair as the tears started all over again. Mom rushed to put her arms around her and tried to console her the best she could.

Dad looked old to me for the first time. He looked defeated as he stood there in the doorway with his head bowed. He laid his big hand on Rains shoulder. "I'll look again at first light." Then he turned and left the room.

My heart was breaking for my sister. She loved that dog more than anything.

I got Jackson by his collar and led him from the room. I didn't think Rain needed to see him right now. And I wanted to give him a big hug. I led him out the front door onto the porch. Dad was sitting in his rocker with his pipe lit, staring off into the dark. His shotgun was propped beside him.

I sat down on the steps with Jackson. I hugged him as he planted kisses all over my face. I was so thankful to have him. I petted and hugged him for a while. Then I thought I should go check on my sister. I stood up to take him out to the barn.

"not tonight," Dad said." I want you to keep him inside tonight."

I stood there for a moment feeling a little confused.

" Go on now", dad said. "Take him up to your room tonight."

"But Rain",I started..

"Rain will be on the couch with your mom tonight" dad said, without changing his stare.

" Now take him on up to bed", he said.

I was still confused, but I knew to do as dad said. I took Jackson back into the front door and led him up to my bedroom.

Rain had quietened down in the kitchen. Now all I could here was mom talking softly. But they were to far away for me to make out what she was saying. I was just glad that Rain was beginning to feel better.

Chapter 7

I woke the next morning to Jackson laying across me feet. The events of the night before came rushing back. Max was still missing! I looked over and seen that Rains bed had not been slept in. I needed to get up and see what was going on. Maybe dad would let me go help him look for Max.

I went downstairs to find Rain asleep on the couch and mom sleeping in dads chair. They must have been up pretty late.

I heard some movement in the kitchen. Dad must be out there. I wanted to go find out if there was any news on Max, and ask what he wanted me to do with Jackson today.

I entered the kitchen just as dad was putting some eggs in the frying pan. He looked up as I entered the room.

"Biscuits are in the stove", he said. "And the eggs will be done shortly."

" Sounds good", I told him, taking a seat at the table. Dad was still wearing the same clothes from the night before, and it looked like he hadn't even shaved. His hair was still tousled from the little bit of sleep he got before Max went missing.

" Do you want me to let Jackson run lose as usual today"? I asked him.

Dad was busy scrambling the eggs, as he spoke. "After breakfast, I want to take him with me."

'To look for Max"? I asked. Why would he want to take Jackson with him to look for Max?

"Yes," Dad responded. "I think he may be able to lead me to his brother. I tried last night, but he was just to excited too track him".

I was just about to ask if I could go when my uncles came in the kitchen door.

" Pour yourselves a cup of coffee and we'll have some breakfast before we get started," dad said.

Mom and Rain came into the kitchen looking like neither had slept. Rain's eyes were red and swollen. She must have cried herself to sleep I thought.

We all ate the breakfast dad had fixed. mom got up to clean the table as the men went out on the porch. This was my chance to ask dad if I could tag along.

I stepped out onto the porch to see my uncles loading their guns. This looked serious. I couldn't ever remember having both of my uncles here at the same time unless it was a Holiday.

" Can I go with you"? I asked dad. ' I'm good with a gun now and I know most of the places the dogs would go", I added.

" Not this time, Raven," dad said, as he checked his scope. "I want you staying in the house with your mom and your sister. I don't want any of you outside at all", he told me. "Now run on up and bring Jackson down, he told me".

I brought Jackson down to the front porch to dad. Dad bent over and clipped a lead to his collar. Just as dad bent over I noticed that he had his shotgun over one shoulder and his bow over the other. The arrows hung in a quiver down the center of his back. The was a handgun fastened to his right leg and a big knife strapped to his ankle. Both of my uncles were dresses similarly. Seeing all of this frightened me. They expected to have to fight something or they wouldn't be dressed this way. Now I feared for all of them. It looked like they were going off to fight a war instead of look for a lost dog.

I watched as the left the porch and walked across the yard with my Jackson leading the way. I said a silent prayer for Max.

Dad and his brothers had been gone all day. The orange from the setting sun was starting to spread across the living room floor.

Mom and I had kept ourselves busy in the kitchen while Rain just sat and stared at the TV. I had wondered a few times if she even knew it was on. She finally fell asleep from sheer exhaustion.

As Rain slept in dad's big chair, mom and I went out to the kitchen to have a cup of coffee.

I sat down at the table as mom poured the steaming hot coffee. "Do you think they will be home tonight"? I asked.

Mom looked at me and gave the best fake smile she could manage. "I'm sure they are fine. Now you stop that worrying", she told me.

We sat in silence for a while, both of us focused on our coffee cups as if they held the answers to all of our questions.

After waiting all day and late into the evening. We all three fell asleep in the living room. We were startled awake by something big hitting the side of the house!

Mom jumped to her feet and ran to the front door. I think she assumed it was dad. She opened the front door and looked out. There was nothing there. As she was looking out the front door something hit the back side of the house near the kitchen! I jumped up and raced to the kitchen as mom quickly closed the front door. I opened the kitchen door to see a huge tree branch laying on the back porch. Where had that come from? We didn't have any trees near the back porch and there wasn't any wind blowing tonight. As I stood there pondering this, a rock landed at my feet! Mom grabbed me by the shoulder and yanked me backward into the kitchen. She quickly closed the door and locked it.

I stood there in the kitchen shocked and confused. I had never seen mom or dad either one lock a door unless the whole family was leaving. And Mom never locked a door when one of us was still outside. She knew daddy was out there somewhere. Why did she lock the door? Where had that tree branch come from? I turned to ask mom, and saw here standing there looking at me with one finger pressed to her lips signaling me not to speak. A whoop came from the front side of the house.

I froze for a minute wondering what she meant. Rain! She didn't want me to scare Rain. I nodded my head to her to let her know I understood. She smiled a worried smile and reach for my hand. We both walked back into the living room.

Rain was still curled up in dad's chair.

Mom turned the TV on and we sat back down. Soon the sound of a sitcom filled the living room. Luckily, it was one of Rains favorites, so it wasn't long until she was engrossed in the show and smiling.

We had watched a couple hours of TV when Mom finally stood up" Would anyone like some sweet tea"? She asked. Stretching her arms over her head as if to get the kinks out of her back.

" Yes", "I would," I told her. "And a piece of that apple pie too please"? I asked.

Mom turned to look at Rain. "That sounds good", she said with a small smile.

I was thrilled to see my sister smiling and wanting food.

The three of us ate in front of the TV, still waiting on dad.

Just as the faintest hint of light began to show in the sky, we heard dad's boots on the front porch.

Mom jumped up and raced to the front door flinging it open. There stood dad with Jackson on the lead and Max flung over his shoulder!

"Oh my God!" exclaimed mom.

" I jumped up and grabbed Jackson's lead". As dad asked mom for a blanket.

Mom brought the blanket back, placing it in front of the fireplace. Dad walked over and knelt down with a very lifeless Max. I just stood there with my hands on Rains shoulders. I didn't even know if the dog was alive. I didn't see any traces of blood on him so that had to be a good thing.

Luke and John had stepped into the room as dad gently lay Max on the blanket.

' Is he alive"? Mom asked softly, with her hand over her mouth.

"Barely", dad responded. I think he has internal damage. I can't find a place on him."

"What should we do"? Mom asked.

"There is nothing we can do", dad replied. It is all up to him. We're going to leave him here by the fire, and pray. That's all that can be done."

Rain walked over and knelt down by Max. She began to stroke him and speak softly. " You've got to get better Max", She said. " I love you and I don't want to be without you. Please get better." Her tears dropped onto his coat. " I love you so much", she whispered. There was the faintest flicker of tail movement. He knew she was talking to him.

Dad turned to his brothers and thanked them for their help. They both shook his hand and gave mom hugs before they left.

Dad said we all should go to bed and sleep for a while. We headed toward the stairs as Jackson lay down on the blanket beside his brother. Max's eyes remained closed.

It was late afternoon before I woke up. At first, I was disoriented. What day was this? What had happened? Then It all came flooding back to me. I lay there listening for any sounds of movement in the house. Rain was still asleep in her bed. I was glad to see this. My little sister had been through a lot. The rest would be good for her.

I pushed the covers back and slowly slipped from my bed. I wanted to go check on Max. and I needed to take care of Jackson. He had to be hungry.

As I walked down the stairs, I was looking toward the fireplace. Jackson was sitting on the blanket beside Max and blocking my view of him. I was completely in the living room before I could see that Max was now laying curled up and he had his eyes open!

"Rain"!
"Mom"!
"Dad"!
I screamed. "Max is awake"!

Rain was running down the stairs in just seconds, followed closely by dad and then mom. Rain rushed over to him falling on her knees. Max didn't lift his head so Rain bent all the way down to kiss him on his head." I love you so much"! She told him.

Dad knelt down beside Rain and ran his hand down Max's body. "Speak softly to him", dad said. "We don't want him trying to get up just yet."

" Can we offer him food yet"? Mom asked.

" Not just yet", dad replied. "We will start with some water in a bit."

With all the excitement of Max getting better I completely forgot about the things that happened before dad came home. I remembered the tree limb and knew it had to be moved. When I stepped out on the back porch, it was gone. Had I dreamed it?

Dad finally told us that he thought Max had tangled with a bear. He had found him laying beside a tree not far from here, but his collar was missing. It wasn't on him when dad found him so we just assumed it came off during the fight.

Max made a full recovery. But he wasn't the same. He was now very skittish. The least little thing scared him. And he wouldn't leave the yard anymore. If Rain and I went to the river Max no longer followed us. He would only walk a few feet from the front porch. The house was his security now. But that was just fine with us. We all loved him and were thankful to have him back.

Because of the bear that attacked Max, dad had us stay close to the house for the next few months. That was fine with me and Rain, we were both to scared to venture far away,

Chapter 8

Fall and winter passed and the weather began to grow warmer. School wasn't out for the summer just yet and the warm weather was making me restless.

It was a clear Saturday morning with the temperature in the mid seventies. I wanted to finish my chores and go do something fun.

I was shoveling hay out of the horse stalls when Rain came in the barn.

"Hey Rain", I yelled over my shoulder."Do you want to go riding later"? "We could ride the horses up to play in the river".

"Sure", she replied. "Just let me turn the goats out and I'll get the horses ready."

She had the horses saddled and ready to go by the time I finished the stalls. We mounted our horses and left the pasture. I wanted to take the long way to the river today and enjoy the ride. I pointed in the direction we would go and Rain nodded yes. We entered the small trail in the woods with Jackson following along.

As we rode I was seeing all of the signs of an early Summer. The spring buttercups were already being replaced by ferns.

Rain and I rode along in silence. Both of us lost in our own thoughts. I was enjoying all of the sounds and smells of the woods. I felt relaxed and content. All was right with the world. I watched as Jackson would catch something on the air and run ahead of us, then he would lose the scent and come back, only to put his nose to the ground and be gone again.

After we had been riding a while I noticed my horse Meredith begin to lay her ears back. And she would turn them periodically letting me know that she heard something. I thought I heard some rustling in the bushes beside us, But the sound was to faint

We were beginning to hear the faintest sound of the river and the air around us was a few degrees color. We were almost there! As we came up the clearing I could see that there was no one in our spot today. We would have this place all to ourselves!

Rain and I got down off of the horses and led them out into the water. We would scoop up the water with our hands and pour it over the horses.

After cooling them down, Rain and, I tethered them in the shade then went back to the river to have some fun ourselves.

We were splashing and squealing like young girls do when we heard a loud tree break! My mind immediately went back to our berry picking and what I had seen. I had seen a monster! We both froze and listened, our ears perked toward the woods on the lower part. That seemed to be the direction the sound had come from.

" It's OK", I told her. "It was just a dead tree falling."

We heard nothing else, so we played for a while longer, before laying on the bank to dry off. Jackson had gone into the woods a couple of times barking at something, but he always came back shortly after my calling him.

The sun was starting to set lower in the sky now and cast some crazy shadows. I didn't know what time It was but I figured it was about time to go so we didn't worry mom. Just as I stood up to gather my things, from our left, I heard someone's footsteps crunching on the leaves. I froze in place as Jackson gave a low guttural growl. I looked all over the tree line but I couldn't see anything. My heart was racing in my chest!

Rain stood up quietly and gathered her stuff. She stepped next to me and whispered, "Listen".

She motioned toward our right. This was the opposite direction of what I had heard. But she was right. I could hear footsteps crunching the leaves. There was no doubt in my mind that these were human footsteps and there was more than one. Someone was out here with us, and the fact that they were trying to be sneaky shot a bolt of fear through me.

I nodded toward our horses so she would know that we needed to mount up and leave. The horses had begun to dance in place. Head down and tails swatting at unseen insects. They were reacting to an unseen enemy. Jackson was still giving his warning growl that usually meant something or someone was getting to close.

I was putting my things away in my saddle bag as Rain mounted her horse. Just as I reach for the reins there was a horribly loud scream that came from the woods. My heart fell into the pit of my stomach. I had heard this scream before. I was frozen in place by sheer terror. This scream was so loud that I felt it in my chest as much as I heard it! Jackson bolted and ran for the woods.

The fear of him running brought me out of my catatonic state. I was remembering what had happened to Max! I screamed for him from the top of my lungs, causing whatever was in the woods to scream again. My horse reared up yanking the reins from my hand! In a split second she was gone! Running back down the trail. Rain's horse was going nuts and she was holding on for dear life. I stepped up to calm her horse and climbed up on the back. I wrapped my arms tightly around Rain and yelled, "Go"! I couldn't worry about Jackson. I had to get us home. I had to get us safe.

Just as those words left my lips, it stepped out of the woods, The monster I had always heard about stepped right out in front of us. It was about nine feet tall and covered with dark brown hair. It's face and hands looked like worn black leather. And it's eyes felt like they could look right through me. They were darker than any I had ever seen.! My heart leaped up into my chest and my reality fell away. In that split second of time, my mind completely shut down. I was losing my grip on reality. The line between fantasy and reality no longer existed.

Rains horse reared up throwing me to the ground, before it let out a horrible whine and bolted back down the trail with Rain barely hanging on. I was now laying at the feet of this monster. I was dazed from the fall I had just taken.

As if in a dream I could hear Jackson barking in the distance. A dark cloud was beginning to fill my eyesight and the monster was becoming hazy. Jackson screamed from another world.

When I woke up, I was lying on the river bank. I was confused as to why I was here. How long had I been asleep? I sat up and looked around. Where was Rain? I saw her towel lying in the clearing about eight feet away and I remembered what had happened. My heart froze with fear. Jackson! Jackson had screamed! I wanted to yell for him, but I was afraid the monster would come back. I had to call him. I couldn't just leave him here. With more fear than I had ever felt before, I called out to him. I waited and listened for even the faintest response. But the woods were completely silent. I slowly stood up. My legs felt like jello, and I wondered if they could even support me. I called out to Jackson again. I didn't want to leave him But I was afraid if I yelled to much the monster, the Kecleh-Kudleh, would come back for me.

I was facing the area where this thing had stepped out of the woods. I heard the faint rustling of leaves and my heart jumped. Could it be? Did I dare hope?
It was Jackson! I knew it had to be Jackson, the noise was to faint for it to be the monster!

As I eagerly watched the tree line, a bloody Jackson came staggering out of the woods. His Back leg and tail were completely gone. One ear had been ripped from his head and part of his upper lip was gone. He took a few staggering steps and collapsed. I screamed at the top of my lungs! Nooooooo! Jackson had been trying to save us! He had been trying to help! This couldn't be happening. This was just a horrible dream. My mind could not comprehend what my eyes were seeing. Nothing this horrible could ever happen. I had to wake up! I had to make myself wake up! As I stood there on wobbly legs this monster came back out of the woods. It looked right at me and rolled its lips back, like a mean dog would, showing me its teeth. It growled a low mean growl. I saw it's lips quiver with the outward rush of air. It bent down and picked up Jackson by his front leg. Jackson's bloody body dangled from its massive hand. My dog let out a small whimper and went silent. This thing growled at me again, stepped back into the woods and was gone. I was more scared than I have ever been in my life. My mind was reeling not being able to process what had just happened.

Rain? Where was Rain? I remembered her horse bolting and her hanging on as tight as she could. I was sure her horse had ran back to the barn. I felt a moment of relief knowing Rain was safe. I looked down at the ground and tried to concentrate on walking.

I would put one foot in front of the other and walk out of here. This thing may get me before I got out of the woods, but I had to try, I had to try to get home. I heard a distant whoop that caused my blood to go cold. There was another whoop that followed not far from me. They were coming! I had to run! As I ran I thought of my horse.

Meredith? Meredith had ran at the first sight of the monster. I was sure she was back safely in the barn by now. That is what the horses did if spooked. They ran back to safety, Just like what I was doing now. As my mind frantically tried to make sense of what was happening, I heard that horrible scream again. It was just a few feet inside the woods. Another one across the river answered it back! They were flanking me again! My blood went cold and I began to run for the trail on rubbery legs. As I ran I could feel my strength coming back and I began to place sure footsteps on the trail. I rounded the bend and came to an abrupt stop almost falling in the process. There lay Meredith with her throat half eaten and her guts were all spilling out. Her whole stomach was laid wide open. I could only think that this looked like it did when you gutted a rabbit. So much blood. There was just so much blood. Then the smell of it hit me. I put my hand over my mouth and nose, letting out a primal whimper.

It felt like my heart had just been ripped from my chest and I was horrified at the carnage that lay before me. I had never experienced such horror and my mind did a jump. I actually felt the small flutter inside my head, a small tickle like butterfly wings. It was my accepting that what my eyes were seeing was real. This was all actually happening. I was heaving from running so hard and now I was going to get sick. I turned away and got sick a few times, knowing I still had to get out of these woods. I passed my horse slowly, keeping my eyes diverted. Then I broke into a full run again. I was half way home when I met my dad coming up the trail on Thunder. Dad had his shotgun over one shoulder and his bow over the other. He reaches down with one hand and in a single, swift movement pulled me up behind him. I wrapped my arms around him tightly and began to sob into his back as he turned the horse and urged him into a run back down the trail.

When we got to the house dad stopped Thunder close to the front porch. Mom was standing there waiting for us. When she saw me she rushed down the steps to help me down from the horse.

"Where is Rain"? Dad urgently called from the saddle.

I spun around to face him. "I thought she was home, I stammered. Her horse bolted and ran for home. The hot tears were spilling down my cheeks. She was holding on as tightly as she could" I finished.

"Lady Bug came back", dad said. Rain wasn't with her.

I felt my heart drop to the pit of my stomach. This nightmare wasn't over.

Dad yelled for mom to call Luke and John, and then he was gone. Racing back up the trail as fast as Thunder could run. I watched my dads back moving fluidly with the racing horse, knowing he was going to fight the Kecleh-Kudleh. I was wondering if I would ever see my dad again. And what kind of repercussion would come from the Kecleh-Kudleh, your Bigfoot.

Mom guided me into the house then went to the kitchen to call my uncles. I sank down into the couch just feeling empty. I had no more emotions. I just felt empty.

Mom came back out to the living room and sat down beside me. I soon heard my uncles trucks hurrying up the driveway.

"Are they taking the horses"? I asked.

"I believe they will", Mom responded. 'It will just be faster that way".

"Meredith is dead," I told her with a sob.

I heard mom give a quick gasp. She reach out and took my hand. " Look at me", mom said.

I looked up into my mother's anxious face."I need you to tell me what happened" "Raven, I need to know where your sister is."

I told mom the whole story. From the time we left the yard to the time dad lifted me up on Thunder. I had to stop a few times and just breath as my mind reeled over the facts that were coming out of my mouth. By the time I finished my mother was crying silently.

At day break dad and my uncles came back for some food. As my mom put food in a bag, dad had me call down to the neighbors and ask to borrow three fresh horses. He told me not to give them any explanation, just ask to borrow the horses.

They all three climbed into Johns truck and were gone again.

Mom and I napped in the living room and then went out to feed the animals. That was all of the chores we did was just to feed and water the animals.

Where could Rain be? Was she hurt? Was she just lost? Why couldn't she find her way home? She knew these woods as well as I did. I knew in my heart that something had to be keeping her from coming home.

On the fourth day, Mom and I were busy in the kitchen preparing food because we knew dad would be back for it. That is all we saw of him, was when he stopped in for food. Dad was well beyond the point of exhaustion, but he wouldn't stop. If necessary, he would die out there looking for Rain.

We heard him yell from the front of the house, his deep voice splitting the silence like lightening. "Paula"! Mom let out a whimper and dropped the pan of biscuits on the counter spilling them everywhere. We both ran for the front door. Dad was standing in the front yard with Rain in his arms. Her head hung back at a funny angle and her shorts were gone. She was dirty from head to toe.

Mom rushed to them crying openly now. She brushed Rains hair away from her face, kissing her dirty cheeks.

" Let's get her in the house", dad said. You could see the exhaustion on him and my uncles. None of them had slept for days. Dad told them to come on in and sleep here but they decided to go home. Mom and dad both thanked them before they left.

Dad lay Rains lifeless body on the couch and mom knelt on the floor beside her.

Rain was breathing, but it was a slow labored breath.

Mom cleaned her up and put her pajamas on her. Rain never woke up. It was as if she were just in a deep sleep. Mom stayed by her side. Rubbing her hands and feet with a traditional ointment. And praying quietly.

After two days, my sister woke up.

"Mom and I were sitting with her when her eyes began to flutter. "Rain", mom said, taking her hand. "Rain baby, it's mama" she said. Rain slowly opened her eyes and looked at mama, then her eyes moved over to me. Her face held no expression at all. No sign of any recognition.

"You're OK now", mom told her. "You're safe at home baby". Rain did not respond.

That day we went up to the river, was the last day any of us ever heard Rains voice.

Rain was taken to different doctors that ran many tests, but none of them could explain why Rain could no longer speak.

The Kecleh-Kudleh, your Bigfoot, took my dog, my horse, and my sister's voice.

Chapter 9

All of this happened thirty five years ago. And now, almost everyday I read where someone is feeding them. These things are like any other wild animal. You feed them and everything is good. But one day, when you stop, they will hunt for their own food. And they wont be hunting in the woods. They will be hunting you. I know a lot of people wont believe me, but I accepted that long before I chose to speak out.

I went over to visit my sister today. As I drove up the long driveway I could smell the pine trees and damp earth. I drove up to the old oak tree in the front yard and stopped. Rain was sitting in a rocking chair on the front porch . She looked over at my car and smiled.

Mom came out of the house, wiping her hands on a dish towel, as I walked up the steps. She gave me a smile and a big warm hug. I returned her hug and sat down in the chair near Rain. I reach out and took her hand as she smiled at me.

Mom went back into the house, as Rain and I sat there holding hands and rocking. I thank God everyday for my sister.

" It sure is pretty out here, isn't it" Rain responded with a smile and a nod. She has not spoken one word since that day she and I took the horses to the river. Rain will not leave the house now. If taken to a doctor, she must be sedated. She will only venture as far as the porch. And just as the sun begins to go down, she will go inside, locking the door behind her.

I often wish my sister could tells us what happened to her while she was gone. But a part of me is thankful that she can't.

Dad has grown old, can no longer tend the farm, so all of the animals have been gone for a while. He grows a small garden now, just enough for the three of them. I get up here as often as I can and go fishing with him. But I choose not to live on the reservation. To much has happened and to much is kept secret. I can no longer justify some of the things that go on inside the reservation and I feel that I can not be a part of it. I was raised to be honest and true to my heart. Mom and dad understand my reasoning, but I'm sure a part of them is saddened that I chose to turn away from my people. If I am to live in peace and have peace within myself, then I can no longer be a part of my people. I can not accept secrets and lies, no matter how they try to justify that what they are doing is right.

I have told my story and now I must wait. I will wait for the repercussions and I will accept them with truth in my heart.

They are real.
They are out there.
They are watching you.

Made in United States
Troutdale, OR
11/09/2023